D0189886

THE TAMING OF THE SHREW

William Shakespeare

TECHNICAL DIRECTOR Maxwell Krohn
EDITORIAL DIRECTOR Justin Kestler
MANAGING EDITOR Ben Florman

SERIES EDITORS Boomie Aglietti, Justin Kestler
PRODUCTION Christian Lorentzen, Camille Murphy

WRITERS Patrick Gardner, Brian Phillips
EDITORS Dennis Quinio, Jesse Hawkes

Copyright © 2002 by SparkNotes LLC

All rights reserved. No part of this book may be used or reproduced in any manner
whatsoever without the written permission of the Publisher.

SPARKNOTES is a registered trademark of SparkNotes LLC.

This edition published by Spark Publishing

Spark Publishing
A Division of SparkNotes LLC
120 Fifth Avenue, 8th Floor
New York, NY 10011

Any book purchased without a cover is stolen property, reported as "unsold and
destroyed" to the Publisher, who receives no payment for such "stripped books."

02 03 04 05 SN 9 8 7 6 5 4 3 2 1

Please send all comments and questions or report errors to
feedback@sparknotes.com.

Library of Congress information available upon request

Printed and bound in the United States

RRD-C

ISBN 1-58663-389-9

INTRODUCTION:
A PROLOGUE
FROM THE
BARD

Brave scholars, blessed with time and energy,
    At school, fair Harvard, set about to glean,
From dusty tomes and modern poetry,
    All truths and knowledge formerly unseen.
From forth the hungry minds of these good folk
    Study guides, star-floss'd, soon came to life;
Whose deep and deft analysis awoke
    The latent "A"s of those in lit'rary strife.
Aim far past passing—insight from our trove
    Will free your comprehension from its cage.
Our SparkNotes' worth, online we also prove;
    Behold this book! Same brains, but paper page.
If patient or "whatever," please attend,
    What you have missed, our toil shall strive to mend.

CONTENTS

NOTE: This SparkNote refers to the Norton Shakespeare edition of *The Taming of the Shrew.* Line numbers, scene numbers, spelling of words and of characters' names, and even diction may differ considerably in other editions. In particular, Petruccio's name is often spelled "Petruchio," and Katherine is often called "Katherina."

CONTEXT

THE MOST INFLUENTIAL WRITER in all of English literature, William Shakespeare was born in 1564 to a successful middle-class glove-maker in Stratford-upon-
Avon, England. Shakespeare attended grammar school,
but his formal education proceeded no further. In 1582
he married an older woman, Anne Hathaway, and had three children with her. Around 1590 he left his family behind and traveled to
London to work as an actor and playwright. Public and critical
acclaim quickly followed, and Shakespeare eventually became the
most popular playwright in England and part-owner of the Globe
Theater. His career bridged the reigns of Elizabeth I (ruled 1558–
1603) and James I (ruled 1603–1625), and he was a favorite of both
monarchs. Indeed, James granted Shakespeare's company the greatest possible compliment by bestowing upon its members the title of
King's Men. Wealthy and renowned, Shakespeare retired to Strat-
ford and died in 1616 at the age of fifty-two. At the time of Shakespeare's death, literary luminaries such as Ben Jonson hailed his
works as timeless.

Shakespeare's works were collected and printed in various editions in the century following his death, and by the early eigh-
teenth century his reputation as the greatest poet ever to write in
English was well established. The unprecedented admiration gar-
nered by his works led to a fierce curiosity about Shakespeare's life,
but the dearth of biographical information has left many details of
Shakespeare's personal history shrouded in mystery. Some people
have concluded from this fact and from Shakespeare's modest
education that Shakespeare's plays were actually written by
someone else—Francis Bacon and the Earl of Oxford are the two
most popular candidates—but the support for this claim is over-
whelmingly circumstantial, and the theory is not taken seriously by
many scholars.

In the absence of credible evidence to the contrary, Shakespeare
must be viewed as the author of the thirty-seven plays and 154 son-
nets that bear his name. The legacy of this body of work is immense.
A number of Shakespeare's plays seem to have transcended even the
category of brilliance, becoming so influential as to affect pro-
foundly the course of Western literature and culture ever after.

The Taming of the Shrew is one of Shakespeare's earliest comedies, and it shares many essential characteristics with his other
romantic comedies, such as *Much Ado About Nothing* and *A Midsummer Night's Dream*. These characteristics include lighthearted
and slapstick humor, disguises and deception, and a happy ending in
which most of the characters come out satisfied. The lightearted-
ness of these romantic comedies contrasts sharply with the darker
humor and deeper characterization of Shakespeare's later plays,
both comic and tragic. The youthfulness of the playwright can be
seen in the whimsical spirit of the early plays. Like the other romantic comedies, *The Taming of the Shrew* focuses on courtship and
marriage, but, unlike most of them, it devotes a great deal of attention to married life after the wedding. The other comedies usually
conclude with the wedding ceremony itself.

A play focusing on the concerns of married life would have
seemed particularly relevant to English audiences of the Renaissance period. Theirs was a society concerned with marriage in general, thanks in part to Henry VIII's separation of England from the
Catholic Church in 1534 in order to secure a divorce that the pope
had refused to grant him. Henry's troubles highlight one important
aspect of Elizabethan marriages among the upper class: they were
most often arranged for money, land, or power, rather than for love.
Moreover, unless you were the king of England, the late sixteenth
and early seventeenth centuries offered few ways out of an unhappy
marriage. Thus, the resolution of marital disputes became an important topic in the popular literature of the era.

Of particular worry to this society were "shrews" or
"scolds"—that is, cantankerous or gossipy wives, who resisted or
undermined the assumed authority of the husband within a marriage. A large number of sermons, plays, and pamphlets of the
time address related topics: the taming of shrews by their husbands or the public punishment of scolds by, for example, repeatedly dunking them in a river. Part of this body of literature took a
very diplomatic attitude toward women, although much of it was
extremely misogynistic. In some of this literature, it is difficult to
distinguish between behavior that is being parodied and behavior
that is presented as an ideal. This ambiguity may also be found in
The Taming of the Shrew, which manages to lampoon chauvinistic
behavior while simultaneously reaffirming its social validity. The
play celebrates the quick wit and fiery spirit of its heroine even
while reveling in her humiliation.

PLOT OVERVIEW

IN THE ENGLISH COUNTRYSIDE, a poor tinker named Christopher Sly becomes the target of a prank by a local lord. Finding Sly drunk out of his wits in front of an alehouse, the lord has his men take Sly to his manor, dress him in his finery, and treat him as a lord. When Sly recovers, the men tell him that he is a lord and that he only believes himself to be a tinker because he has been insane for the past several years. Waking in the lord's bed, Sly at first refuses to accept the men's story, but when he hears of his "wife," a pageboy dressed in women's clothing, he readily agrees that he is the lord they purport him to be. Sly wants to be left alone with his wife, but the servants tell him that a troupe of actors has arrived to present a play for him. The play that Sly watches makes up the main story of *The Taming of the Shrew*.

In the Italian city of Padua, a rich young man named Lucentio arrives with his servants, Tranio and Biondello, to attend the local university. Lucentio is excited to begin his studies, but his priorities change when he sees Bianca, a beautiful, mild young woman with whom Lucentio instantly falls in love. There are two problems: first, Bianca already has two suitors, Gremio and Hortensio; second, Bianca's father, a wealthy old man named Baptista Minola, has declared that no one may court Bianca until first her older sister, the vicious, ill-tempered Katherine, is married. Lucentio decides to overcome this problem by disguising himself as Bianca's Latin tutor to gain an excuse to be in her company. Hortensio disguises himself as her music teacher for the same reason. While Lucentio pretends to be Bianca's tutor, Tranio dresses up as Lucentio and begins to confer with Baptista about the possibility of marrying his daughter.

The Katherine problem is solved for Bianca's suitors when Hortensio's friend Petruccio, a brash young man from Verona, arrives in Padua to find a wife. He intends to marry a rich woman, and does not care what she is like as long as she will bring him a fortune. He agrees to marry Katherine sight unseen. The next day, he goes to Baptista's house to meet her, and they have a tremendous duel of words. As Katherine insults Petruccio repeatedly, Petruccio tells her that he will marry her whether she agrees or not. He tells Baptista, falsely, that Katherine has consented to marry him on Sunday. Hearing this claim, Katherine is strangely silent, and the wedding is set.

3

On Sunday, Petruccio is late to his own wedding, leaving Katherine to fear she will become an old maid. When Petruccio arrives, he is dressed in a ridiculous outfit and rides on a broken-down horse. After the wedding, Petruccio forces Katherine to leave for his country house before the feast, telling all in earshot that she is now his property and that he may do with her as he pleases. Once they reach his country house, Petruccio continues the process of "taming" Katherine by keeping her from eating or sleeping for several days—he pretends that he loves her so much he cannot allow her to eat his inferior food or to sleep in his poorly made bed.

In Padua, Lucentio wins Bianca's heart by wooing her with a Latin translation that declares his love. Hortensio makes the same attempt with a music lesson, but Bianca loves Lucentio, and Hortensio resolves to marry a wealthy widow. Tranio secures Baptista's approval for Lucentio to marry Bianca by proposing a huge sum of money to lavish on her. Baptista agrees but says that he must have this sum confirmed by Lucentio's father before the marriage can take place. Tranio and Lucentio, still in their respective disguises, feel there is nothing left to do but find an old man to play the role of Lucentio's father. Tranio enlists the help of an old pedant, or schoolmaster, but as the pedant speaks to Baptista, Lucentio and Bianca decide to circumvent the complex situation by eloping.

Katherine and Petruccio soon return to Padua to visit Baptista. On the way, Petruccio forces Katherine to say that the sun is the moon and that an old man is really a beautiful young maiden. Since Katherine's willfulness is dissipating, she agrees that all is as her husband says. On the road, the couple meets Lucentio's father, Vincentio, who is on his way to Padua to see his son. In Padua, Vincentio is shocked to find Tranio masquerading as Lucentio. At last, Bianca and Lucentio arrive to spread the news of their marriage. Both Vincentio and Baptista finally agree to the marriage.

At the banquet following Hortensio's wedding to the widow, the other characters are shocked to see that Katherine seems to have been "tamed"—she obeys everything that Petruccio says and gives a long speech advocating the loyalty of wives to their husbands. When the three new husbands stage a contest to see which of their wives will obey first when summoned, everyone expects Lucentio to win. Bianca, however, sends a message back refusing to obey, while Katherine comes immediately. The others acknowledge that Petruccio has won an astonishing victory, and the happy Katherine and Petruccio leave the banquet to go to bed.

Character List

Katherine The "shrew" of the play's title, Katherine, or Kate, is the daughter of Baptista Minola, with whom she lives in Padua. She is sharp-tongued, quick-tempered, and prone to violence, particularly against anyone who tries to marry her. Her hostility toward suitors particularly distresses her father. But her anger and rudeness disguise her deep-seated sense of insecurity and her jealousy toward her sister, Bianca. She does not resist her suitor Petruccio forever, though, and she eventually subjugates herself to him, despite her previous repudiation of marriage.

Petruccio Petruccio is a gentleman from Verona. Loud, boisterous, eccentric, quick-witted, and frequently drunk, he has come to Padua "to wive and thrive." He wishes for nothing more than a woman with an enormous dowry, and he finds Kate to be the perfect fit. Disregarding everyone who warns him of her shrewishness, he eventually succeeds not only in wooing Katherine, but in silencing her tongue and temper with his own.

Bianca The younger daughter of Baptista. The lovely Bianca proves herself the opposite of her sister, Kate, at the beginning of the play: she is soft-spoken, sweet, and unassuming. Thus, she operates as Kate's principal female foil. Because of her large dowry and her mild behavior, several men vie for her hand. Baptista, however, will not let her marry until Kate is wed.

Baptista Minola Baptista is one of the wealthiest men in Padua, and his daughters become the prey of many suitors due to the substantial dowries he can offer. He is good-natured, if a bit superficial. His absentmindedness increases when Kate shows her obstinate nature. Thus, at the opening of the play, he is already desperate to find her a suitor, having decided that she must marry before Bianca does.

Lucentio A young student from Pisa, the good-natured and intrepid Lucentio comes to Padua to study at the city's renowned university, but he is immediately sidetracked when he falls in love with Bianca at first sight. By disguising himself as a classics instructor named Cambio, he convinces Gremio to offer him to Baptista as a tutor for Bianca. He wins her love, but his impersonation gets him into trouble when his father, Vincentio, visits Padua.

Tranio Lucentio's servant. Tranio accompanies Lucentio from Pisa. Wry and comical, he plays an important part in his master's charade—he assumes Lucentio's identity and bargains with Baptista for Bianca's hand.

Gremio and Hortensio Two gentlemen of Padua. Gremio and Hortensio are Bianca's suitors at the beginning of the play. Though they are rivals, these older men also become friends during their mutual frustration with and rejection by Bianca. Hortensio directs Petruccio to Kate and then dresses up as a music instructor to court Bianca. He and Gremio are both thwarted in their efforts by Lucentio. Hortensio ends up marrying a widow.

Grumio Petruccio's servant and the fool of the play—a source of much comic relief.

Biondello Lucentio's second servant, who assists his master and Tranio in carrying out their plot.

Christopher Sly The principal character in the play's brief Induction, Sly is a drunken tinker, tricked by a mischievous nobleman into thinking that he is really a lord.

ANALYSIS OF MAJOR CHARACTERS

KATHERINE

Widely reputed throughout Padua to be a shrew, Katherine is foul-tempered and sharp-tongued at the start of the play. She constantly insults and degrades the men around her, and she is prone to wild displays of anger, during which she may physically attack whomever enrages her. Though most of the play's characters simply believe Katherine to be inherently ill-tempered, it is certainly plausible to think that her unpleasant behavior stems from unhappiness. She may act like a shrew because she is miserable and desperate. There are many possible sources of Katherine's unhappiness: she expresses jealousy about her father's treatment of her sister, but her anxiety may also stem from feelings about her own undesirability, the fear that she may never win a husband, her loathing of the way men treat her, and so on. In short, Katherine feels out of place in her society. Due to her intelligence and independence, she is unwilling to play the role of the maiden daughter. She clearly abhors society's expectations that she obey her father and show grace and courtesy toward her suitors. At the same time, however, Katherine must see that given the rigidity of her social situation, her only hope to find a secure and happy place in the world lies in finding a husband. These inherently conflicting impulses may lead to her misery and poor temper. A vicious circle ensues: the angrier she becomes, the less likely it seems she will be able to adapt to her prescribed social role; the more alienated she becomes socially, the more her anger grows.

Despite the humiliations and deprivations that Petruccio adds to her life, it is easy to understand why Katherine might succumb to marry a man like him. In their first conversation, Petruccio establishes that he is Katherine's intellectual and verbal equal, making him, on some level, an exciting change from the easily dominated men who normally surround her. Petruccio's forcible treatment of Katherine is in every way designed to show her that she has no real choice but to adapt to her social role as a wife. This adaptation must be attractive to Katherine on some level, since even if she dislikes the

7

role of wife, playing it at least means she can command respect and consideration from others rather than suffer the universal revulsion she receives as a shrew. Having a social role, even if it is not ideal, must be less painful than continually rejecting any social role at all. Thus, Katherine's eventual compliance with Petruccio's self-serving "training" appears more rational than it might have seemed at first: by the end of the play, she has gained a position and even an authoritative voice that she previously had been denied.

PETRUCCIO

The boastful, selfish, mercurial Petruccio is one of the most difficult characters in *The Taming of the Shrew*: his behavior is extremely difficult to decipher, and our interpretation of the play as a whole changes dramatically depending on how we interpret Petruccio's actions. If he is nothing more than a vain, uncaring, greedy chauvinist who treats marriage as an act of domination, then the play becomes a dark comedy about the materialism and hunger for power that dictate marriages under the guise of courtly love. If, on the other hand, Petruccio is actually capable of loving Kate and conceives of taming her merely as a means to realize a happy marriage, then the play becomes an examination of the psychology of relationships.

A case can be made for either interpretation, but the truth about Petruccio probably lies somewhere in between: he is unabashedly selfish, materialistic, and determined to be his wife's lord and master, but he also loves her and realizes on some level that domestic harmony (on his terms, of course) would be better for her than her current life as a shrew in Padua. To this extent, Petruccio goes to alarming lengths to impose his mastery on Kate, keeping her tired and hungry for some time after their marriage, but he also insists on framing this treatment in a language of love, indicating his eagerness for Kate to adapt to her rightful, socially appointed place and his willingness to make their marriage a happy one. Above all, Petruccio is a comic figure, an exaggerated persona who continually makes the audience laugh. And though we laugh with Petruccio as he "tames" Kate, we also laugh at him, as we see him satirize the very gender inequalities that the plot of *The Taming of the Shrew* ultimately upholds.

LUCENTIO

Just as Bianca is Katherine's foil—her opposite—the intrepid, lovesick Lucentio serves as a foil for Petruccio throughout the play. Lucentio reflects the sort of idyllic, poetical view of love that Petruccio's pragmatism dismisses: Lucentio is struck by love for Bianca at first sight, says that he will die if he cannot win her heart, and subsequently puts into motion a romantic and fanciful plan to do so. Whereas love in the play is often mitigated by economic and social concerns, Lucentio is swept up in a vision of courtly love that does not include the practical considerations of men like Petruccio. Throughout much of the play, then, Lucentio and Bianca's relationship appears to be refreshing and pure in comparison to the relationship between Petruccio and Katherine. Petruccio's decision to marry is based on his self-proclaimed desire to win a fortune, while Lucentio's is based on romantic love. Moreover, while Petruccio devotes himself to taming his bride, Lucentio devotes himself to submitting to and ingratiating himself with his. While Petruccio stages his wedding as a public spectacle, Lucentio elopes with Bianca.

The contrast between Lucentio and Petruccio distinguishes *The Taming of the Shrew* from other Elizabethan plays. Through Lucentio and Bianca, the play looks beyond the moment when the romantic lovers are wed and depicts the consequences of the disguises and subterfuges they have charmingly employed to facilitate their romance. Once the practical business of being married begins, Lucentio's preoccupation with courtly love seems somewhat outmoded and ridiculous. In the end, it is Petruccio's disturbing, flamboyant pragmatism that produces a happy and functioning marriage, and Lucentio's poeticized instincts leave him humiliated when Bianca refuses to answer his summons. Love certainly exists in the world of *The Taming of the Shrew*, but Lucentio's theatrical love, attractive though it is, appears unable to cope with the full range of problems and considerations facing married couples in adult life.

CHARACTER ANALYSIS

Themes, Motifs & Symbols

Themes

Themes are the fundamental and often universal ideas explored in a literary work.

Marriage as an Economic Institution

As a romantic comedy, the play focuses principally on the romantic relationships between men and women as they develop from initial interest into marriage. In this respect, the play is a typical romantic comedy. However, unlike other Shakespearean comedies, *The Taming of the Shrew* does not conclude its examination of love and marriage with the wedding. Rather, it offers a significant glimpse into the future lives of married couples, one that serves to round out its exploration of the social dimension of love.

Unlike in Romeo and Juliet, inner emotional desire plays only a secondary role in *The Taming of the Shrew*'s exploration of love. Instead, *The Taming of the Shrew* emphasizes the economic aspects of marriage—specifically, how economic considerations determine who marries whom. The play tends to explore romantic relationships from a social perspective, addressing the institutions of courtship and marriage rather than the inner passions of lovers. Moreover, the play focuses on how courtship affects not just the lovers themselves, but also their parents, their servants, and their friends. In general, while the husband and the wife conduct the marriage relationship after the wedding, the courtship relationship is negotiated between the future husband and the father of the future wife. As such, marriage becomes a transaction involving the transfer of money. Lucentio wins Bianca's heart, but he is given permission to marry her only after he is able to convince Baptista that he is fabulously rich. Had Hortensio offered more money, he would have married Bianca, regardless of whether she loved Lucentio.

THE EFFECT OF SOCIAL ROLES ON
INDIVIDUAL HAPPINESS

Each person in the play occupies a specific social position that carries with it certain expectations about how that person should behave. A character's social position is defined by such things as his or her wealth, age, gender, profession, parentage, and education; the rules governing how each of them should behave are harshly enforced by family, friends, and society as a whole. For instance, Lucentio occupies the social role of a wealthy young student, Tranio that of a servant, and Bianca and Katherine the roles of upper-class young maidens-in-waiting. At the very least, they are supposed to occupy these roles—but, as the play shows, in reality, Kate wants nothing to do with her social role, and her shrewishness results directly from her frustration concerning her position. Because she does not live up to the behavioral expectations of her society, she faces the cold disapproval of that society, and, due to her alienation, she becomes miserably unhappy. Kate is only one of the many characters in *The Taming of the Shrew* who attempt to circumvent or deny their socially defined roles, however: Lucentio transforms himself into a working-class Latin tutor, Tranio transforms himself into a wealthy young aristocrat, Christopher Sly is transformed from a tinker into a lord, and so forth.

Compared with Katherine's more serious anguish about her role, the other characters' attempts to circumvent social expectations seem like harmless fun. However, the play illustrates that each transformation must be undone before conventional life can resume at the end of the play. Ultimately, society's happiness depends upon everyone playing his or her prescribed roles. Through the motif of disguise, the play entertains the idea that a person's apparel determines his or her social position, but it ultimately affirms that this is not the case. A servant may put on the clothes of a lord, but he remains a servant, one who must return to his place, as we see with Tranio. Likewise, Lucentio must reveal his subterfuge to his father and to Baptista before moving forward with Bianca. Kate's development over the course of the play is basically determined by her gradual adaptation to her new social role as wife. She complies with Petruccio's humiliating regimen of taming because she knows on some level that, whether she likes the role of wife or not, she will be happier accepting her social obligations than living as she has been at odds with everyone connected to her. In fact, the primary excitement in *The Taming of the Shrew* stems from its permeable social boundaries, crisscrossed continually by those who employ a disguise or a clever lie. In the end, however, the conventional order reestablishes itself, and those characters who harmonize with that order achieve personal happiness.

MOTIFS

Motifs are recurring structures, contrasts, or literary devices that can help to develop and inform the text's major themes.

DISGUISE

Disguise figures prominently in *The Taming of the Shrew*: Sly dresses as a lord, Lucentio dresses as a Latin tutor, Tranio dresses as Lucentio, Hortensio dresses as a music tutor, and the pedant dresses as Vincentio. These disguises enable the characters to transgress barriers in social position and class, and, for a time, each of them is successful. The play thus poses the question of whether clothes make the man—that is, whether a person can change his or her role by putting on new clothes. The ultimate answer is no, of course. In *The Taming of the Shrew*, society involves a web of antecedents that are always able to uncover one's true nature, no matter how differently one wishes to portray oneself. Tranio, disguised as Lucentio, needs only to bump into Vincentio, and his true identity surfaces. As Petruccio implies on his wedding day, a garment is simply a garment, and the person beneath remains the same no matter what disguise is worn.

DOMESTICATION

The motif of domestication is broadcasted in the play's title by the word "taming." A great part of the action consists of Petruccio's attempts to cure Katherine of her antisocial hostility. Katherine is thus frequently referred to as a wild animal that must be domesticated. Petruccio considers himself, and the other men consider him, to be a tamer who must train his wife, and most of the men secretly suspect at first that her wild nature will prove too much for him. After the wedding, Petruccio and Katherine's relationship becomes increasingly defined by the rhetoric of domestication. Petruccio speaks of training her like a "falcon" and plans to "kill a wife with kindness." Hortensio even conceives of Petruccio's house as a place where other men may learn how to domesticate women, calling it a "taming-school."

FATHERS AND THEIR CHILDREN

The several father/child relationships in the play—Baptista/Bianca, Baptista/Katherine, Vincentio/Lucentio—focus on parents dealing with children of marriageable age and concerned with making good matches for them. Even the sham father/son relationship between the disguised pedant and the disguised Tranio portrays a father attempting to make a match for his son, as the pedant attempts to negotiate Tranio's marriage to Bianca. Through the recurrence of this motif, Shakespeare shows the broader social ramifications of the institution of marriage. Marriage does not merely concern the future bride and groom, but many other people as well, especially parents, who, in a sense, transfer their responsibility for their children onto the new spouses.

SYMBOLS

Symbols are objects, characters, figures, or colors used to represent abstract ideas or concepts.

PETRUCCIO'S WEDDING COSTUME

The ridiculous outfit Petruccio wears to his wedding with Kate symbolizes his control over her. Simply by wearing the costume, he is able to humiliate her. It may be shameful for Kate to be matched to someone in such attire, but she knows she has no choice if she does not wish to become an old maid. She consents to let the ceremony proceed, even with Petruccio dressed like a clown, and thus yields to his authority before the wedding even begins.

The outfit also symbolizes the transient nature of clothing. Petruccio declares that Kate is marrying him, not his clothes, indicating that the man beneath the attire is not the same as the attire itself. Thus, Lucentio, dressed as a tutor, cannot escape the fact that he must return to his true identity. By the same token, when Kate plays the role of a dutiful wife, she remains, essentially, Kate.

THE HABERDASHER'S CAP AND TAILOR'S GOWN

The cap and gown that Petruccio denies Katherine, despite the fact that she finds them truly appealing, symbolizes yet again his power over her. The outfit functions as a kind of bait used to help convince Kate to recognize and comply with Petruccio's wishes. Only he has the power to satisfy her needs and desires, and this lesson encourages her to satisfy him in return.

SUMMARY & ANALYSIS

INDUCTION I–II

SUMMARY: INDUCTION I

Outside an alehouse somewhere in the English countryside, a drunk beggar named Christopher Sly argues with the Hostess over some glassware he has broken in his inebriated clumsiness. While the Hostess leaves to find the local authorities, Sly passes out, and soon a lord returning from the hunt discovers him. This lord decides to have a bit of fun with the sleeping beggar and orders his servants to take Sly back to his house and treat him as if he were a lord—to put him in a bed, place rings on his fingers, set a banquet for him, and so on. His huntsmen agree that doing so would be an excellent jest, and they bear Sly offstage.

A troupe of players arrives, seeking to offer the lord their services. The lord welcomes them to spend the night at his home, but he warns them that they must not laugh at the strange behavior of the other lord for whom they will perform. Then the lord tells his serviceman to go to Bartholomew, the lord's pageboy, and instruct him to put on the attire of a lady and play the part of Sly's wife. The lord wants the disguised Bartholomew to pretend to be overjoyed to see that Sly has recovered from his insanity and to say that Sly has madly insisted that he is a poor beggar for the past seven years.

SUMMARY: INDUCTION II

Back at the house, the servants place Sly in the lord's bed with fine clothes and jewelry, and the lord outfits himself as one of the servants. When Sly awakes, they present him with good wine and food and tell him that he is their master. He protests that he remembers being a poor tinker (a mender of pots), and they explain that this memory is but the result of a madness from which he has suffered for fifteen years. They put on quite a show, pleading and wailing in feigned distress at his continued illness, but Sly remains skeptical. However, when his "wife" is mentioned, Sly is finally convinced. Overjoyed that their master's memory has returned, the servants try to entertain him. Sly attempts to dismiss the servants so that he can sleep with his wife (who is actually the disguised page, Bartho-lomew), but his wife explains apologetically that his physicians have ordered her to stay out of his bed for another night or two, lest his madness return. The players arrive to perform for the enjoyment of Sly and his wife. The play that they perform constitutes the rest of *The Taming of the Shrew.*

ANALYSIS: INDUCTION I–II

The Induction is an unusual feature of this play. None of Shakes-peare's other plays begins with a framing story, in which a full five-act play is performed within another play. The story and the charac-ters involved in the Induction have nothing directly to do with the main play, and after its introduction this story is only reintroduced briefly and never fully developed. Another play from the mid-1590s, however, entitled *The Taming of a Shrew* and probably based on Shakespeare's work, features Sly's commentary through-out the main story. At the end of the main story, Sly declares his intention to tame his own wife as Petruccio has tamed Katherine.

Critics disagree about why Shakespeare begins *The Taming of the Shrew* with the Induction. The play proper could obviously stand on its own, but the story of the lord's practical joke on Chris-topher Sly does reinforce one of the central themes of the main play. Sly's story dramatizes the idea that a person's environment and the way he or she is treated by others determines his or her behavior—an idea that Katherine's story in the main play also illustrates. The lord thrusts Sly into a playacting world and portrays his new role as coming into being through no will of his own. The lord's huntsman emphasizes this when asked if Sly would fall for the deception and forget himself. "Believe me, lord, I think he cannot choose," he responds (Induction.I.38). The huntsman's words could apply equally well to Katherine. Controlled by two wealthy and powerful men—her father, Baptista, and her suitor, Petruccio—Katherine is forced to play the part of a wife, a social role that she initially rejects. The implication that Katherine, like Sly, "cannot choose" suggests that she is as much a plaything of Petruccio as Sly is of the lord.

The Induction also introduces the topic of marriage into the play. Sly resists all the servants' attempts to convince him that he is a lord until they tell him that he has a wife, at which point he immediately reverses himself: "Am I a lord? And have I such a lady?" (Induc-tion.II.66). Shakespeare emphasizes Sly's about-face by switching

Sly's speech pattern to blank verse (unrhymed lines of iambic pentameter, spoken primarily by Shakespeare's noble characters). Before, Sly had spoken only in prose. The humor of the situation is obvious: though Sly is at first preoccupied with making sense of his outrageous change of circumstances, as soon as he discovers that he might be able to be physically gratified, he immediately stops caring whether his situation is real or fantastical, commanding his wife to "undress you and come now to bed" (Induction.II.113). Shakespeare here playfully introduces a number of ideas that receive further attention later in the play, such as the idea that marriage is something that people use for their own benefit rather than a reflection of some deeper truth about the married couple. Moreover, the roles of class, gender, and marital status, which in ordinary life seem to be set in stone, here become matters of appearance and perception, subject to manipulation by the characters or the playwright. Indeed, the Induction primes Shakespeare's audience to think critically about what he will present next.

Act I, scene i

Summary: Act I, scene i

A young man named Lucentio arrives in Padua with his manservant, Tranio. Lucentio was educated in Pisa and Florence and has come to Padua to further his studies at its famous university. As he announces to Tranio, he is young and eager to learn new things. Tranio pleads that they should not forget the pleasures of life in their academic pursuits. The noisy entrance of a crowd interrupts their discussion.

The crowd is composed of Baptista Minola; his daughters, Katherine and Bianca; and Bianca's two suitors, older men named Hortensio and Gremio. Most of the noise comes from Katherine, who seems to be caught up in a rage, screaming and cursing at everyone present. When Baptista informs the suitors that they are free to court Katherine, but that he will not allow Bianca to marry before Katherine does, they respond that no one would ever marry a devil like her. Katherine threatens them with violence in return. Amid all the noise, though, Lucentio takes particular notice of Bianca, who behaves much more mildly than her sister. After Baptista leaves with his daughters, Hortensio and Gremio agree that they have but one option: to look for someone to wed Katherine. However, they are not optimistic about their chances of finding a willing man. In the meantime, they say, they will also look for a schoolmaster for Bianca—Baptista had mentioned that he was looking for one, and they hope to earn favor with Bianca's father by helping him.

The old men walk away, and Lucentio gushes to Tranio that he has fallen in love with Bianca and is determined to court her. Knowing that he cannot do so publicly, given Baptista's forbiddance, he resolves to woo her in secret. He suddenly recalls that Hortensio and Gremio mentioned procuring a schoolmaster, and he decides to disguise himself as a teacher in the hope that by tutoring Bianca he will be able to declare his love for her and win her heart. Tranio, for his part, will pretend to be Lucentio and study at the university. Biondello, Lucentio's other servant, arrives in a timely fashion and agrees to help with the deception.

At this point, the main story—which is being presented as a play for Christopher Sly—fades for a moment, and Sly reemerges. He declares briefly that he is enjoying this entertainment, but he implies that he would prefer to be left alone with his wife.

ANALYSIS: ACT I, SCENE I

Shakespeare wastes no time in establishing who is the "shrew" of the play's title. Within a few lines, the first scene introduces the public perception of Katherine as hateful and sharp-tongued, characteristics considered hallmarks of the shrew in Shakespeare's time. In their disparaging rejections of Katherine, Hortensio and Gremio specify what they dislike about her: she is "too rough" (I.i.55), and they want mates "of gentler, milder mould" (I.i.60). After watching Katherine for only a few seconds, Tranio remarks, "That wench is stark mad," indicating just how far Katherine's behavior diverges from the norm (I.i.69). Throughout the play, the characters contrast their ideas of the "shrew" with their differing ideas of the "ideal wife." Here, we see that the two suitors value a mild disposition in a wife, and thus they greatly prefer Bianca to Katherine, despite the ladies' comparable dowries.

The indignant denunciation of Katherine by Hortensio and Gremio illustrates the social biases and assumptions that Shakespeare intends to humorously explore throughout the play, specifically, society's expectations concerning a woman's role in a marriage. Hortensio and Gremio represent the then-conventional view that a woman should sacrifice her individuality in submission to her husband. Certainly, this expectation plays a part in their decision to prefer the mild, submissive Bianca to the fiery Katherine. Katherine's temperament threatens to upset the accepted order, in which the wife bows to the authority of the husband. Shakespeare poses the basic thematic question of the play in the very first scene: does a happy and stable marriage depend upon a woman's sacrifice of her own will? Such a sacrifice seems to be unacceptable to Katherine, who vociferously defends her independence: "What, shall I be appointed hours, as though belike I knew not what to take and what to leave? Ha!" (I.i.102–104).

Most people in Shakespeare's society believed that the woman should submit to her husband, and yet they did not necessarily expect the wife to sacrifice all of her independence and sense of self. Likewise, we should not be too hasty to accuse Hortensio and Gremio of outright misogyny at this point in the play. Judging from the dialogue thus far, their dislike of Katherine may seem a natural reaction to Katherine's behavior. The qualities she first presents are a violent temper, jealousy in the face of Bianca's preferential treatment, and disrespect for her father. On the other hand, like the other male characters in the play, Hortensio and Gremio do adopt a very patronizing attitude toward Katherine. They speak about her in the third person rather than addressing her directly—perhaps because they are simply terrified of what she would say back to them if they addressed their words to her. If we compare Katherine to the heroines of Shakespeare's later comedies, such as Rosalind in *As You Like It*, Portia in *The Merchant of Venice*, Viola in *Twelfth Night*, or Beatrice in *Much Ado About Nothing*, Katherine's situation appears extremely anomalous. All of those later heroines are outspoken and independent, and the happy resolution of those plays depends upon whether or not the male characters listen to what the heroines say. Katherine's rage reflects her struggle to be recognized as a person rather than treated as a pet or an object.

The subplot between Lucentio and Bianca also shows subtle signs of objectifying women. While the romance between these two young lovers will seem a sweet and beautiful thing compared to the violent struggle between Petruccio and Katherine, Lucentio does not necessarily view Bianca as his equal. On the contrary, he sees her mostly as a prize to be won: "I burn, I pine, I perish, Tranio / If I achieve not this young modest girl" (I.i.149–150). If Bianca merely represents something for Lucentio to "achieve," then his view of her lacks depth. Lucentio has fallen in love with her appearance, and

Tranio remarks that Lucentio has looked so persistently at the pretty Bianca that he has missed the main point of the situation.

ACT I, SCENE II

SUMMARY: ACT I, SCENE II

A brash young man named Petruccio, newly arrived in Padua, goes with his servant Grumio to see Hortensio, whom he knows from Verona. Grumio and Petruccio become embroiled in a comic misunderstanding at the door, but eventually Hortensio comes down to greet Petruccio and ask why he is in Padua. Petruccio responds that, upon his father's death, he set out to look for a wife, hoping to marry a rich man's daughter and thereby augment his family fortune. Hortensio, determined to find a potential suitor for Katherine so that he himself may marry Bianca, recognizes his opportunity and decides to convince Petruccio to marry the shrew. Being a friend, he first tries to offer a warning about her, but Petruccio does not care about her behavior. He pays attention to one thing only—the fact that she has a rich father. Full of confidence, he tells Hortensio to lead him to the shrew. Hortensio, for his part, plans to disguise himself as a schoolmaster so that he can court Bianca secretly.

Gremio and Lucentio enter on their way to Baptista's house, interrupting Hortensio and Petruccio. Lucentio has already disguised himself as a schoolmaster and has presented himself to Gremio, who gladly agrees to have him tutor Bianca. Gremio brags to Hortensio that he has found a schoolmaster for Bianca, unaware of the fact that Lucentio will be courting the girl himself. Hortensio then tells Gremio the good news—that Petruccio wishes to woo Katherine. Gremio can hardly believe it, but Petruccio confidently claims that he will be victorious.

At this point, Tranio enters, disguised as Lucentio, with Biondello as his servant. He very conspicuously asks the suitors to direct him to the house of Baptista Minola, vaguely implying that he might be interested in one of the women there. Hortensio and Gremio have a hard time restraining their anger, for now there will be three competing suitors for Bianca. Lucentio, of course, has arranged for Tranio to make this entrance in order to distract Hortensio and Gremio and give him more time for his own wooing. Tranio persuades the suitors that they can all be friends while they compete for Bianca, and he wins their good graces by offering to buy them a

SUMMARY & ANALYSIS

drink. The whole company considers this an excellent suggestion, and they all depart together.

ANALYSIS : ACT I, SCENE II

The reader is bombarded in the first half of the scene by Petruccio's overbearing personality. Several character traits rapidly reveal themselves: he is quick to anger but also quick to laugh, as he displays in his frequent quarreling with his servant Grumio. He has a coarse personality, but he is educated well enough to spout classical references and has a quick wit. Also, he loves money above all else, which explains his enthusiasm for courting Katherine. As Grumio remarks, if given enough gold, Petruccio would happily marry a puppet, a clothing ornament, or a toothless hag with venereal diseases. These are superficial motives, to be sure, but Petruccio proclaims them proudly, and Shakespeare uses his proclamations to introduce another dimension to the play's exploration of marriage: the idea that marriage is essentially an economic activity, intended to consolidate fortunes and facilitate the distribution of inheritances. Petruccio, having been left some money by his own father, knows that he can strike it rich if he allows himself to be "bought" as a husband.

Money is not Petruccio's only driving force. As more characters warn him about Katherine's harsh tongue, he begins to view wedding her as a challenge rather than simply a moneymaking opportunity. Living with the shrew, he says, could not possibly be worse than enduring the hardships of war or the sea. Gremio says that subduing Kate would be a heroic challenge, comparing the task to one of the labors of Hercules, even as he discourages Petruccio from undertaking it. In their minds, Katherine has apparently transformed from an insubordinate woman into either a monster in need of subjugation or a tempest that has to be withstood. In fact, they give her the title "Katherine the curst" (I.ii.122). The more the men talk about her, the worse the report of her behavior becomes.

In her absence, Katherine's situation becomes a bit clearer. People talk about her more than they listen to her, and the more people gossip about her, the more they dislike her. She wields her tongue to defend herself in the only way she can, but this only earns her greater disrepute. After all, in the earlier scene between Katherine and the two suitors, Katherine becomes angry after Gremio insults her, although we do not know what transpired before their entrance onstage. At any rate, this scene clarifies the general bias of the men and elicits some sympathy for Katherine. In many ways, the men are more interested in competing in tests of machismo and going to the pub than they are in the thoughts or feelings of the women whom they wish to woo.

ACT II, SCENE I

SUMMARY: ACT II, SCENE I

Chaos rules at Baptista's house the next morning as Katherine chases Bianca, cursing at her in a fury. Katherine has tied Bianca's hands together and is trying to beat her sister because Bianca will not tell her which of the suitors she prefers. When Baptista comes in to try to break up the fight, he only angers Katherine more by showing that he favors Bianca. Both sisters leave in a huff, just before a group of visitors enters to see Baptista.

The group is composed of the gentlemen who were on their way to the pub at the end of the last scene: Gremio with Lucentio (dressed as a schoolmaster), Petruccio with Hortensio (likewise dressed as a schoolmaster), and Tranio (dressed as Lucentio) with Biondello (dressed as his servant). The introductions begin in a whirlwind of deception. Petruccio starts off, bluntly as always, by asking Baptista for the opportunity to see Katherine. In exchange, he offers a music instructor for her, the disguised Hortensio, whom he introduces as Licio. Baptista accepts the present and intends to tell Petruccio as kindly as possible that Petruccio must be crazy to want to see Katherine, when Gremio, who cannot stand being upstaged, interrupts him. Gremio presents his own schoolmaster, the disguised Lucentio, whom he calls Cambio, a master of classical languages. Baptista accepts the gift and then hears from Tranio, who, pretending to be Lucentio, presents his own gift of books and a lute, in exchange for the permission to see and woo Bianca.

The two phony schoolmasters leave to ply their trades on Bianca, while Petruccio presses Baptista further for information about Katherine. After confirming that a substantial dowry will accompany his successful wooing of Katherine, Petruccio assures Baptista of his abilities. Hortensio cuts him off by returning, his head now bleeding—apparently, when Hortensio attempted to teach Katherine how to play the lute, she promptly took the

SUMMARY & ANALYSIS

instrument and smashed it over his head. Undaunted, Petruccio waits for Baptista to send Katherine out to see him. He decides to adopt the tactic of calling her "Kate" and good-naturedly contradicting everything she says.

Abrasive as always, Katherine tears into Petruccio from the moment he sets foot in her room. Petruccio's quick wit, though, proves equal to hers, and Katherine, used to skewering the slower-witted men by whom she is surrounded, finds his aptitude for sparring highly frustrating. They engage in a lengthy verbal duel with elaborate puns, each one constructing a new metaphor from the other's comments—Kate's puns generally insult or threaten, but Petruccio twists them into sexual innuendo. Eventually, she becomes so enraged that she hits him, but he continues the game just the same, saying that he will marry her whether or not she is willing: "will you, nill you, I will marry you" (II.i.263).

When Baptista, Gremio, and Tranio enter to check on Petruccio's progress, he claims that they have already agreed upon Sunday as the wedding day. Kate, shocked, contradicts him, but he ignores her objections and insists to the other men that Katherine cannot keep her hands off him. Strangely, Kate remains silent after this remark, and when Petruccio again claims that they will marry on Sunday, she says nothing, and they both leave.

After recovering from the shock of the hasty arrangement they have just witnessed, Gremio and Tranio immediately move to the matter of Bianca, who suddenly will be available after Sunday. Baptista says that whichever of the suitors can best ensure that Bianca will be provided for when she is a widow—in other words, whichever has the greatest wealth—may have her hand. Having assumed the false, unknown identity of Lucentio, Tranio is able to claim that he has limitless funding and simply guarantees ten times whatever Gremio offers. Baptista agrees to award Bianca to Lucentio as soon as his father can guarantee the wealth that he has claimed. Tranio, confident of his ability to play the part of Lucentio, believes he can produce Lucentio's father as well.

ANALYSIS: ACT II, SCENE I

Although the turning point of the action in a Shakespearean play usually occurs in the third act, here, in Act II, we already witness an emotional turning point for Kate when she fails to refute Petruccio's assertion that they are engaged. Her silence at the end of this scene is remarkable. She has always used her tongue liberally to get her way, and here, when Petruccio seems to force marriage upon her, a decision that will affect the rest of her life, she lapses into silence. As before, when Baptista is present, the men ignore Kate, talking about her, not to her. In the same way, Petruccio treats her like she doesn't exist when telling the others of their wedding plans. In fact, Petruccio thinks so little of what Kate replies that Gremio, fearing that Petruccio's presumptuous confidence will impede his own chances of marrying Bianca, reiterates what Kate initially says to him: "Hark, Petruccio, she says she'll see thee hanged first" (II.i.292). Inexplicably, when Petruccio persists, she actually complies.

Kate's compliance with Petruccio's decree may surprise us, but if we consider her as essentially misunderstood by the other characters, her behavior may appear more understandable. The men view her as a shrew, but they care very little about the origins of her shrewish nature. Nor do they wonder why Kate chooses to maintain her behavior. If her temper results from her frustration with the dim-witted qualities of the men around her, one easy explanation for her acceptance of Petruccio would be that he is her equal in wit and will-power. Indeed, compared to the other suitors who simply run from Kate's temper, Petruccio fires a countering shot at each and every one of her arrows. Petruccio displays an admirable wit, and, in this verbal duel of puns and double entendres, we see quintessential Shakespeare inventiveness and linguistic skill. On the other hand, Petruccio does not respect Kate, or at least he pretends to disrespect her for the sake of the game. It seems strange that Kate's independent personality would be willing to accept someone who gives her just as little credit as did the other suitors merely because he can match her wit.

At the beginning of the scene, though, Kate shows that she may have another motive for complying with Petruccio. When fighting with Bianca, she admits that she is jealous because of the fact that her sister is being courted and will probably soon marry. She says to Baptista: "She [Bianca] is your treasure, she must have a husband. / I must dance barefoot on her wedding day, / And for your love to her lead apes in hell" (II.i.32–34). (Leading apes in hell refers to the lot of women who die old maids, unmarried.) Here, Kate appears to be frustrated by the fact that her biological clock is ticking, but she finds herself caught in a vicious circle: she hates the suitors because they do not want to marry her, and men will not marry her because she makes it so obvious that she hates them.

Perhaps Petruccio's indefatigable nature has broken the cycle, or it may be that he is the first man to speak kind words to her, even if he did not truly mean them.

Whereas Hortensio and Gremio make it very clear when they are put off by Kate's sharpness, Petruccio amiably covers it up with praise: "For she's not froward, but modest as the dove. / She is not hot, but temperate as the morn" (II.i.285–286). After Petruccio invokes this simile, Kate's resistance falters. It will return, but Petruccio clearly did not miss the mark with his strategy, which capitalizes on her need for acceptance. In this scene, Kate shows that she is doubly miserable in her existence as an unmarried girl, having alienated herself from the society she despised. It may be that marriage represents a new beginning for Kate, a chance to take on a new social role and possibly find a more satisfying way to integrate herself into her surroundings.

Act III, scene i

Summary: Act III, scene i

It is now Saturday, the day before Katherine is scheduled to wed Petruccio. Lucentio and Hortensio, in their respective disguises as Cambio and Licio, are "instructing" Bianca somewhere in Baptista's house, and the scene begins with the two of them battling for her exclusive attention. Bianca clearly has begun to form a preference, and she ends the dispute by declaring that she will hear her Latin lesson from Lucentio first, while Hortensio tunes his instrument.

During the Latin lesson, with Hortensio out of hearing range, Lucentio conveys his true intentions to Bianca through a mock translation of a Latin paragraph. She replies to him, in the same way, that she distrusts him, and yet she does not hide the fact that she is taken with her young suitor. Hortensio tries to break in at intervals, but Bianca sends him off to tune again until she has finished her conversation with Lucentio.

Lucentio concludes and Hortensio returns to try his own hand at wooing Bianca. He gives her a sheet with a "gamut," or scale, of notes on it, with romantic words cleverly inserted to indicate his true intention. Hortensio's words take a different tone, though. While Lucentio was confident and coy, Hortensio pleads almost pitifully: "show pity, or I die" (III.i.76). Bianca resists his attempt more directly, failing to give the playful glimmer of hope she afforded Lucentio. Before Hortensio can respond, a servant enters, calling upon Bianca to prepare for her sister's wedding the next day.

Lucentio also leaves, and Hortensio, alone, considers the signals he received from Bianca. He sees clearly that Lucentio is infatuated with Bianca. But he does not yet know what her intentions are, and he suspects that his own chances might be slim. Preparing for the possibility of rejection, his former enthusiasm dwindles, and he tells himself that he will simply find another wife if Bianca proves unwilling.

ANALYSIS: ACT III, SCENE I

Despite the unorthodox presence of the Induction and the story of Christopher Sly, the narrative form of *The Taming of the Shrew* is generally extremely straightforward. It follows the two plots initiated in Act I, scene i: the main plot, involving Katherine's wooing and marriage, and the subplot, involving Bianca's wooing and marriage. This scene offers a diversion from the main plot by turning to the subplot—the wooing of Bianca by her competing suitors.

In Act III, scene i, the play continues to verbally excite as well as explore deeper aspects of love and marriage. Like the argument between Petruccio and Kate in the last scene, the exchange between Lucentio and Bianca displays Shakespeare's considerable skill with puns. It also subtly explores the idea of women in marriage again, this time by contrasting how Lucentio and Hortensio treat Bianca.

The scene employs its fair share of humor. Lucentio's mock Latin lesson pokes fun at the fact that foreign languages are often more compact than English. He translates a ridiculously long English phrase from one or two Latin words: "'Simois,' I am Lucentio, 'hic est,' son unto Vincentio of Pisa," and so forth (III.i.31–32). Hortensio's wooing is just as clever. He uses the scale of notes and their syllable names to convey a series of puns: "B—mi—Bianca, take him for thy lord," with the play on "Be my Bianca," and so forth (III.i.73).

The scene provides more than just clever comedy, however. It establishes the foundation, or perhaps the lack of foundation, of Lucentio and Bianca's love. In contrast to the previous oppositional scene between Petruccio and Kate, the courting here is much more effortless. Lucentio does not have to work as hard as Petruccio did. Bianca expresses some misgivings because she does not know

SUMMARY & ANALYSIS

Lucentio, but she makes it clear that she already prefers him to Hortensio. In many ways, it seems natural for two young, attractive, and sympathetic characters of the play to come together, but this quick and easy match has consequences later on.

ACT III, SCENES II–III

SUMMARY: ACT III, SCENE II
On Sunday, outside Baptista's house, everyone has gathered for the wedding of Kate and Petruccio. The groom, however, is late, and Baptista has begun to worry. Kate frets that Petruccio habitually woos women only to leave them standing at the altar, and she runs off in tears. Just then, Biondello rushes in to announce that the groom is on his way, dressed in a ridiculous, mismatched, and shabby costume, riding up the street on an old, broken-down horse riddled with diseases. Grumio rides at his side, similarly attired. When Petruccio finally arrives, the crowd, horrified, sees that Biondello's description was accurate. Baptista begs him to change into a more fashionable outfit before marrying Kate, in order to avoid further public humiliation. Petruccio says he will do no such thing and rides off to find Kate at the church. Most of the crowd follows in a kind of horrified fascination.

SUMMARY: ACT III, SCENE III
Tranio and Lucentio stay behind, alone. They briefly discuss the status of their plan to win Bianca. Tranio informs his master that they must find a father for him, and Lucentio suggests that the simplest solution may be for them to elope. They do not speak for long before Gremio returns to tell the story of what happened at the marriage. Apparently, Petruccio swore at the altar, struck the priest, threw food, and, in general, proved such an embarrassment that Gremio felt compelled to leave early. The marriage has been completed nonetheless, and the rest of the company soon arrives. However, before they can even begin the wedding feast, Petruccio announces that he must leave at once and take Kate with him, not even giving her time to receive congratulations from her friends and family. At this ridiculous suggestion, Kate tries to draw the line, saying she will leave only when she wishes, but Petruccio remains as persistent as ever. He says that since she is now his wife, he claims her as his property, and, pretending to defend her from jealous thieves, exits

quickly with her and Grumio. The rest of the party can only watch in amazement and laugh at the day's events, wondering how two such people could ever put up with one another. They resume the wedding feast, and Baptista moves to discuss the marriage of Bianca to Lucentio.

ANALYSIS: ACT III, SCENES II–III

In this scene, Petruccio makes it clear that although he has won Kate's hand in marriage, his efforts to tame her are far from complete. Apparently, he has every intention of contradicting her will at every point, even after she has consented to marry him. Now we can see that he doesn't want just her dowry—he really wants a tamed wife. By embarrassing her with his ridiculous costume, crass behavior in the church, and their abrupt exit, he robs her of her dignity even as he overcomes her resistance. He almost seems to mock the fact that she has allowed herself to be wed, making her wish that she could retract the decision. She laments, "I must forsooth be forced / To give my hand opposed against my heart" (III.ii.8–9).

This scene raises the question of whether Kate, like Sly, has any agency in her situation. It returns to the theme of authority in marriage and to the foreshadowing exhibited during the play's Induction. Kate's proven capability of standing up to her father and the other suitors, through words and even violence if necessary, does not manifest itself here with Petruccio. Surely, if she did not wish to marry Petruccio, she would have found a way to resist—she could simply have refused to go to the church or to take the vows once there. Even when she does offer resistance—for instance, when Petruccio demands that they leave immediately after the wedding—she does not respond with the same vigor. Kate does exert some agency by choosing not to fight, but she appears to make this choice because she is cowed by Petruccio's unyielding stance. Thus, if Kate is powerless to stop the actions of others upon her, just as Sly is, then it seems that there will be little equality in this marriage. Petruccio completely subjugates Kate's will. Indeed, Petruccio speaks his most misogynistic lines of the play in this scene as he prepares to pull Kate away from the marriage feast: "She is my goods, my chattels. She is my house, / My household-stuff, my field, my barn, / My horse, my ox, my ass, my anything" (III.iii.101–103).

Petruccio's words are not, however, spoken in all seriousness. First, they are not his original thoughts—they are a list of a man's

SUMMARY & ANALYSIS

possessions from the Bible's Ten Commandments, which Petruccio simply relates to his new wife. By quoting precisely from another text, Shakespeare creates the possibility that Petruccio speaks with self-conscious irony. Furthermore, in the context of the rest of the scene, his little diatribe appears just like his outlandish outfit—a possibly malicious way to embarrass not only Kate but everybody else there. Petruccio's outlandish, exaggerated pronouncement of the social convention of women's inferiority might be interpreted as a satire of the idea that a woman is really a man's property. Petruccio's ironic take on marriage becomes particularly clear when we consider the fact that Petruccio utters his commandments while simultaneously disrupting and dishonoring the traditional Christian marriage rites themselves.

Moreover, Petruccio gives another, very different opinion of married life when Baptista asks him to change his clothes:

> To me she's married, not unto my clothes.
> Could I repair what she will wear in me
> As I can change these poor accoutrements,
> 'Twere well for Kate and better for myself.
>
> (III.ii.110–113)

Here, he is not materialistic but idealistic, not condescending to Kate but self-deprecating—a contrast to the sentiments he expresses in Kate's presence. Petruccio's true feelings might lie somewhere in between these two extremes. He is certainly not willing to treat Kate as an equal, but he also may not be as misogynistic as he appears.

ACT IV, SCENES I–II

SUMMARY: ACT IV, SCENE I

Petruccio and Kate are about to arrive at Petruccio's country house. Grumio arrives first, however, complaining that he has been sent ahead to ensure that the servants prepare for the arrival of their master and his new wife. Curtis, another servant, greets him and hears his tale of the journey from Padua—Kate fell into the mud, Petruccio flew into a rage, and the horses ran away. Grumio then orders Curtis to assemble all the other servants, properly attired and on good behavior. Curtis calls for them, and a few arrive just as Petruccio and Kate return.

Petruccio immediately becomes enraged, claiming that his servants fail to attend him properly. They do their best, but clearly he is not pleased by anything. He demands dinner, and they prepare it as quickly as possible, but he claims that the meat is burned and pushes the whole meal off the table. In the meantime, Kate, visibly tired and hungry, pleads with him to be more patient with the servants. Petruccio cheerfully tells her that he demands much of them for her benefit—his new bride will receive nothing short of perfection, he says, pretending to ignore the fact that his new bride simply needs a hot meal. After taking her off to bed without food, Petruccio returns to the stage alone and announces his intentions. All his actions have been calculated to aggravate Kate and to keep her wanting, for he refers to her as a wild falcon that he must train to obey his call. He intends to prevent her from sleeping by making a fuss about the way the bed is made, just as he did with the food. This, he says, is the best way to "curb her mad and headstrong humour" (IV.i.190).

Summary: Act IV, scene ii

Back in Padua, Tranio (still disguised as Lucentio) and Lucentio (still disguised as the schoolmaster) are trying to conclude their scheme to win Bianca for Lucentio. Hortensio, distraught at having lost Bianca to his rival schoolmaster, takes it upon himself to inform Lucentio that he too is out of luck in his pursuit of Bianca. Tranio plays along, feigning surprise when he sees the real Lucentio and Bianca courting each other during their "lesson." He pretends to be so angry that he decides to foreswear Bianca's charms, and he convinces Hortensio to do the same—thus cleverly removing the competition.

Tranio informs Bianca and Lucentio of these events after Hortensio leaves. Hortensio has decided to marry a wealthy widow instead of Bianca and is leaving to go to Petruccio's to attend "taming-school." He wants to see how Petruccio handles Kate so that he can apply the lessons to his own marriage. Just as Tranio finishes the story, Biondello rushes into the scene with encouraging news: he has just seen a man entering Padua who would make a convincing fake father for Lucentio.

Tranio approaches the newcomer, learning that he is a pedant schoolmaster from Mantua. He then comes up with a story to put the old man in his debt: the dukes of Mantua and Padua, he says, are at odds with each other, and the duke of Padua has proclaimed that anyone from Mantua found in Padua shall be put to death. The pedant, frightened out of his wits, promises a favor to Tranio in exchange for protection. Tranio says that, as it happens, he is in need of someone to act as his father (meaning Lucentio's father, Vincentio), and so they seal the agreement.

ANALYSIS: ACT IV, SCENES I–II

With the beginning of Act IV, the play begins to stick even more closely to the alternating plot/subplot structure that it has followed loosely up to this point: for the next several scenes, the action alternates on a scene-by-scene basis between the Petruccio/Katherine story and the Lucentio/Bianca story. In developing the main plot, this section devotes itself largely to a gradually developing joke in which Petruccio frustrates Kate by using an exaggerated pretense of concern for her comfort to keep her hungry, tired, and generally uncomfortable. In developing the subplot, this section is devoted to the consequences of the increasingly complex series of disguises and deceptions that both enable and complicate Lucentio's courtship of Bianca.

Petruccio's monologue in Act IV, scene i explains most of what transpires in this scene, as he tells the audience of his scheme to bend Kate to his will. He will tame her as the falconer trains his bird, by holding lures out in front of it, just out of reach. All has been planned in his mind in advance: "Thus have I politicly begun my reign," he says, where "politicly" means "with careful calculation" (IV.i.169). Petruccio wishes to bend Kate's hostile temperament into benevolence by turning everything against her—ironically, under the guise of heightened concern for her well-being. He means to "kill [his] wife with kindness" (IV.i.189). Though Petruccio's treatment of Kate is undoubtedly condescending and chauvinistic, it is nevertheless significant that Petruccio decides to "kill" her with kindness rather than with force. By couching his attempts to smooth out Kate's rough temper in language of love and affection, Petruccio both makes himself more sympathetic in the eyes of the audience and opens the way for an actual loving relationship with Kate once she decides to accept her new role as his wife. Had Petruccio simply attempted to dominate his wife forcibly, he would have appeared monstrous to the audience, making a pleasant union impossible.

Though Shakespeare loves to use disguise as a means of transgressing social boundaries, in *The Taming of the Shrew* social roles and social positions are ultimately too binding to escape. This is one

SUMMARY & ANALYSIS

reason why the stakes are so high in Petruccio's "game" with Katherine. Petruccio's monologue indicates the importance of his plan. He understands that despite Kate's independence, her only hope for achieving happiness lies in her ability to adapt to her role as a wife. Otherwise, she will be forced to continue the socially alienated misery of her life as a maiden, out of sync with her role in society. For Petruccio and Katherine, this negotiation is well under way, and, despite their frequent quarreling, it is aided by their obvious attraction to one another. But for the parties involved in the subplot, who continue to deceive themselves and those around them, uncharted waters lie ahead.

In Act IV, scene ii, the subplot nearly reaches complete success. Through the duping of Hortensio and the acquisition of the services of the naïve pedant, all obstacles between Lucentio and Bianca seem to be removed—except, of course, for the fact that the man Baptista knows as Lucentio is really Tranio. This was the fundamental flaw in the plan, which is why Biondello, perhaps the most sensible character in the play, later arranges for the two lovers to elope while Baptista speaks with the pedant. All in all, the whole scheme amounted to little more than an entertaining distraction, since the disguises cannot be maintained forever if Bianca and Lucentio ever wish to fulfill their desires.

From Biondello's news, we see that the ploy has begun to unravel quickly, now that they have finally reached their goal. Once Lucentio and Bianca have married, they must either flee Padua or reveal their ruse, since Baptista soon expects to marry Bianca to the disguised Tranio. It would be no great matter for Lucentio to return to Pisa, or to go elsewhere, since he is wealthy and educated, but for Bianca it would mean abruptly leaving her family, friends, and inheritance. In fact, the young lovers don't have the faintest idea what their married life will be like, since Lucentio has been acting a role from the beginning, and they have had to court each other in secret. They may represent the ideal of young love at first sight, but their love does not seem to be developing in a way that facilitates future growth.

ACT IV, SCENES III–V

SUMMARY: ACT IV, SCENE III

Back in Petruccio's house, Kate has had little food or sleep for several days now, and she entreats Grumio to get her something to eat. He refuses, and, like his master, claims that they are depriving her for her own benefit. Finally, Petruccio and Hortensio bring her a meal. (Hortensio has apparently arrived from Padua sometime in the last few days to educate himself at Petruccio's "taming-school.") Kate has little time to eat before Petruccio's tailor arrives. The tailor has prepared elegant and expensive clothes for their journey back to Baptista's house in Padua. Predictably, Petruccio finds fault with everything that Kate likes, from the cap to the gown, and he blames the tailor for poor craftsmanship. The tailor tries to deflect the blame onto Grumio, but Petruccio and Grumio indignantly force him to leave. Petruccio, however, secretly tells Hortensio to pull the tailor aside and tell him that he will be paid the following day, revealing that Petruccio's distasteful treatment of the tailor is in jest. Petruccio then tells Kate that they will leave at once for Padua in the clothes that they have on, planning to arrive at noon. But, when Kate tells Petruccio that noontime has already past, he angrily responds that, yet again, she is contradicting him. He declares that they will not go that day, and that, when they do go, "[i]t shall be what o'clock I say it is" (IV.iii.189).

SUMMARY: ACT IV, SCENE IV

In Padua, Tranio has properly outfitted the pedant as Vincentio and rehearses his act with him to ensure that their stories match. When Baptista and Lucentio (still disguised as Cambio) enter, the pedant convinces Baptista that he is indeed Lucentio's father, and that he fully approves of the marriage between Bianca and his son. Baptista, the pedant, and Tranio then leave to find a private place where they can discuss the financial details of the marriage.

SUMMARY: ACT IV, SCENE V

Lucentio (disguised as Cambio) returns to the stage with Biondello, who informs him that Baptista has requested that Cambio bring Bianca to dinner. Biondello explains that he has personally arranged for a priest and witnesses to perform a hasty marriage in a church nearby. Lucentio agrees to the plan to elope, and they quickly leave to perform their respective tasks.

ANALYSIS: ACT IV, SCENES III–V

As Act IV, scene iii opens, Kate has clearly been affected by Petruccio's treatment, especially by the excuses he continues to give for his behavior. She complains to Grumio that what particularly infuriates her is that Petruccio torments under the pretense of love. This pretense—not to mention Petruccio's erratic and peremptory behavior—makes it hard for her to react to his actions with her typical anger, since he seems to have the best intentions and to only desire her happiness and comfort. And yet, given Kate's obvious intelligence, it is remarkable that she does not see through Petruccio's facade and realize that he is doing everything simply to frustrate her. Most likely, she does in fact suspect foul play, as she indicates when she says that he torments her "under name of perfect love," implying that the "name" and the reality do not necessarily match (IV.iii.12). She simply does not wish to stand up to him on this point. The play is, after all, a comedy, and we are probably meant to believe that, despite their difficulties, Kate and Petruccio are falling in love, if they have not already done so. Under the comic influence of love, Kate is much less likely to use the full power of her critical thought to see through Petruccio's schemes.

Of course, the attraction between Kate and Petruccio, which exists despite their social inequality and seems to stem from their intellectual equality, is central to our ability to read *The Taming of the Shrew* as something more than merely a troubling chronicle of sixteenth-century spouse abuse. Most readers, as Jean E. Howard notes in her introduction to the play in *The Norton Shakespeare*, "have seen in Kate and Petruccio's relationship an attractive mutuality and vitality they find difficult to reconcile with the idea that the play is simply a lesson in how to subordinate a woman." This sense of an "attractive mutuality" is what enables the play to be funny, but one of the unresolvable complications of *The Taming of the Shrew* is the question of how we should reconcile the apparent love story of the two main characters with Petruccio's obviously cruel treatment of his new wife.

In Act IV, scene iii, Kate once again tries to draw the line: when Petruccio tries to throw away the cap that the tailor made, which she

SUMMARY & ANALYSIS

very much likes. She has had enough and tries to establish an auton-
omous position:

> . . . I trust I may have leave to speak,
> And speak I will. I am no child, no babe.
> . . .
> . . . I will be free
> Even to the uttermost as I please in words.
>   (IV.iii.73–80)

Unfortunately, not even this is enough to get her so much as the cap
in the end. She may be free in words, but her words now fall upon
deaf ears, which is the source of her frustration. Before she met
Petruccio, even though her words were rarely taken well, at least she
could be assured of a reaction to them, and she seemed to take some
delight in the reaction she could wring from men. Now, her words
are ignored even when she removes their edge and asks for the simplest courtesies. Now indeed she cannot choose, for though she is
powerless with Petruccio, she would only endure greater shame if
she fled him and returned to Padua.

Also in Act IV, scene iii, Shakespeare expands his social commentary to include a critique of the importance attributed to clothing.
Petruccio says that it is "the mind that makes that body rich, / And
as the sun breaks through the darkest clouds, / So honour peereth in
the meanest habit" (IV.iii.166–168). By "meanest habit," Pertruc-
cio means poor attire. This speech echoes the sentiment that
Petruccio expressed earlier to Baptista before the wedding, and the
repetition should be noted. The Induction seemed to claim that
clothes and accoutrements could in fact change the man: Sly
changed from a drunkard to a nobleman. Yet, here, Shakespeare
suggests the contrary: the inner nature of a person will eventually
shine through, regardless of the apparel that person chooses to wear.
Indeed, the ruse of Sly's nobility will last only a short time; sooner or
later, he will be put back on the street. It is not clear whether Kate
shares a similar fate, however. Just as the lord dresses Sly, so does
society force Kate to wear the clothing of marriage, both literally
and figuratively. Unlike Sly, Kate is unhappy in the role of the wife,
a role that stifles her independent spirit. In this scene, however, as
Kate's motivations and actions continue to show that she is changing, Shakespeare forces us to question whether the clothing actually
does influence the person within.

ACT IV, SCENE VI–ACT V, SCENE I

SUMMARY & ANALYSIS

SUMMARY: ACT IV, SCENE VI

Petruccio, Kate, and Hortensio journey back to Padua. On the way, Petruccio continues his relentless attempts to coax Kate to submit to his authority as her husband. Though it is midday, Petruccio comments on how brightly the moon is shining, and when Kate responds that the sun is shining, he refuses to continue the journey until she admits that it is the moon. Having no more energy or patience to put up resistance and anxious to return to Padua, Kate concedes. Then, however, Petruccio reverses his claim and says that it is in fact the sun. Hortensio finally persuades Petruccio that he has tamed her, and they continue the journey.

After they have gone a short way, a similar incident occurs. They pass an old man on the same road to Padua, and Petruccio claims that, in fact, the old man is a young maid. Furthermore, he entreats Kate to embrace the maid. This time, Kate immediately obeys, but Petruccio then says she is mistaken, for the maid is really an old man. Kate continues to play along.

The old man turns out to be Vincentio, the true father of Lucentio. He tells the trio that he has come to visit his son in Padua. Petruccio happily tells him of the marriage expected between Bianca and Lucentio and realizes that this will make Vincentio Petruccio's father-in-law. A bit confused, they all continue their journey to Padua together in order to sort things out there.

SUMMARY: ACT V, SCENE I

Back in Padua, Biondello hurriedly takes Lucentio and Bianca to the church, where the priest is ready to marry them. Lucentio is no longer disguised as Cambio the schoolmaster. Just as they leave, Petruccio's party enters along with Vincentio, and they knock on the door of Lucentio's house, where Tranio and the pedant currently reside in their respective disguises. When the pedant answers, Vincentio says that he is Lucentio's father, but the pedant claims to be the true father and calls for the imposter's arrest. Just then, Biondello arrives, turning white when he sees his old master, Vincentio, who recognizes him. Biondello pretends not to notice Vincentio, as Baptista, Tranio, and the pedant come out of the house. Vincentio also recognizes Tranio in Lucentio's clothing, and he is further enraged when Tranio pretends not to know him.

The crowd turns against Vincentio and prepares to escort him to jail, when Lucentio and Bianca, newly married, arrive from the church. Biondello, Tranio, and the pedant take this moment of confusion to run away from the scene, knowing that the game is up. Lucentio can do nothing but beg his father's pardon and disclose the scheme to everyone present. He explains that his deception stemmed from his love for Bianca, which pacifies the two fathers somewhat. Nevertheless, they depart to seek some small revenge on the men who fooled them.

Kate and Petruccio stand in amazement at the proceedings. They follow the rest inside to see the conclusion, but not before Petruccio demands one more thing of his wife. He asks her to kiss him, there in the middle of the street. Initially, Kate refuses, saying she is ashamed to do so. But when Petruccio threatens to turn them around and return to his home, Kate kisses him. Petruccio finally seems satisfied with her, and they go in.

ANALYSIS: ACT IV, SCENE VI–ACT V, SCENE I

These scenes essentially set up the conclusion of both the main plot and the subplot by illustrating the apparent completion of Kate's taming and the unraveling of Lucentio and Tranio's scheme. The disguises that gave great power to Lucentio and to Tranio finally fall away, embarrassing the two young men. No outfit can forever conceal a man's true nature, as Tranio unintentionally reveals in his hasty chiding of Vincentio: "Sir, you seem a sober, ancient gentleman by your habit, but your words show you a madman" (V.i.61–62). Tranio soon receives his just desserts, however, when everyone sees that Vincentio is indeed "a sober, ancient gentleman," and that Tranio is the one whose appearance obscures his true nature. Luckily for the young wedded couple, Lucentio's true nature satisfies Baptista, who allows the marriage to stand. Again, though, how this marriage will progress now that Cambio has changed back into Lucentio remains undetermined. The passionate fire of young, naïve courtship must settle itself into the quiet flame of married life. (Incidentally, the name "Cambio" is also the Italian verb "to change.")

The wall between Kate and Petruccio finally begins to crumble in these two scenes. Petruccio gives the impression that he will never approve of Kate's behavior, for even when she denies what she sees with her own eyes in order to satisfy him, he insults her. After they argue about the shining of the sun and the moon, however, Kate gives him absolute power, even over the definition of reality: "What you will have it named, even that it is, / And so it shall be still for Katherine" (IV.vi.22–23). Petruccio finally seems pleased, but soon he tests her again, asking her to kiss him in public. After her initial resistance and subsequent concession, Petruccio makes a remark that seems to signify the conclusion of the taming: "Is this not well? Come, my sweet Kate. / Better once than never, for never too late" (V.i.130–131). He seems to mean that it is never too late for her to lose her shrewishness for good and become his "ideal" wife.

While frustration certainly plays a part in Kate's final submission, she does not simply allow Petruccio to have his way with her out of desperation. After Kate kisses him in the street, she says, "Now pray thee love, stay" (V.i.129). She calls him "love," not in her usual cynical tone, but with an authentic desire for his company, even despite his recent treatment of her. Finally satisfied, Petruccio responds by calling her "my sweet Kate" (V.i.130). Whereas their previous battles ended in a standoffish tone, here, for the first time, the couple shows genuine, kind feelings for each other. Moreover, the entire exchange concerning the kiss seems more flirtatious than the others, if for no other reason than Petruccio's potentially self-deprecating line when Kate refuses to kiss. He says, "What, art thou ashamed of me?" (V.i.126). Kate actually begins this exchange by illustrating her acceptance of their union by calling Petruccio "Husband" (V.i.122). Ultimately, this short exchange suggests an interpretation of their entire journey as a struggle against the confines of marriage. Kate still obeys Petruccio and calls him husband, and Petruccio still has the ability to make them go home should she refuse. But there, in the middle of the public street, Petruccio asks her to forgo custom, and when she does, they find love.

ACT V, SCENE II

SUMMARY: ACT V, SCENE II

Lucentio throws a banquet to celebrate the three recent marriages in Padua: Petruccio to Kate, Lucentio to Bianca, and Hortensio to the widow he had spoken of before. As they sit around the table eating and chatting, Petruccio and the widow engage in some jesting (mostly at Hortensio's expense). Kate joins in, and she begins to argue with the widow. The argument nearly turns to violence, with the men cheering them on to fight, but Bianca calms them, and the three wives go off together to talk.

Meanwhile, the men begin to chide Petruccio—Baptista, Lucentio, Tranio, and Hortensio still think that Petruccio has been stuck with a vicious shrew, and they give him some grief for it. Petruccio confidently suggests a test to see which of the three new husbands has the most obedient wife. Each of them will send for his wife, and the one whose wife obeys first will be the winner. After placing a significant amount of money on the wager, Lucentio sends Biondello go to get Bianca, confident that she will obey at once. However, Biondello returns to tell them that she is busy and will not come. Hortensio receives a similar response from the widow. Finally, Grumio goes back to get Kate, and she returns at once, to the great surprise of all but Petruccio. Petruccio sends Kate back to bring in the other wives. Again, she obeys. Upon their return, Petruccio comments that he dislikes Kate's hat and tells her to throw it off. She obeys at once. Bianca and the widow, aghast at Kate's subservience, become even further shocked when, at Petruccio's request, Kate gives a speech on the duty that wives owe to their husbands.

In the speech, Kate reprimands them for their angry dispositions, saying that it does not become a woman to behave this way, especially toward her husband. A wife's duty to her husband, she says, mimics the duty that "the subject owes the prince," because the husband endures great pain and labor for her benefit (V.ii.159). She admits that once she was as haughty as Bianca and the widow are now, but that she has since changed her ways and most willingly gives her obedience to her husband. The other men admit complete defeat, and Petruccio leaves victorious—he and Kate go to bed happily, and Hortensio and Lucentio remain behind to wonder at this miraculous change of fates.

ANALYSIS: ACT V, SCENE II

Kate's speech at the end of the play has been the focus of many interpretations. It is, for obvious reasons, abhorrent to many feminist critics, who take issue with Kate's recommendation of total subservience to the husband—she says at different points that the man is the woman's lord, king, governor, life, keeper, head, and sovereign. She also stereotypes women as physically weak and then suggests that they should make their personality mild to match their physique:

> Why are our bodies soft, and weak, and smooth
> . . .
> But that our soft conditions and our hearts
> Should well agree with our external parts?
> (V.ii.169–172)

Petruccio agrees with Kate's description of the ideal relationship. He explains to Hortensio what Kate's obedience will mean: "Marry, peace it bodes, and love, and quiet life; / An aweful rule and right supremacy, / And, to be short, what not that's sweet and happy" (V.ii.112–114). "Right supremacy" suggests that his ideal involves the complete suppression of the wife's will. As a whole, Shakespeare's society took this definition of gender roles for granted. After all, this was a uniformly Christian society that bowed to biblical notions of the husband as the wife's head and the woman as the glory of the man (paraphrasing Ephesians and 1 Corinthians, respectively). In short, Shakespeare's society believed in the hierarchy that Kate earnestly supports in her speech.

Yet, given the fact that the entire play challenges stereotypes and promotes an awareness of ambiguous appearances, both Kate's final speech and Petruccio's views may be open to question. In fact, in the last line of the play, Lucentio implies that Kate, in the end, allowed herself to be tamed: "'Tis a wonder, by your leave, she will be tamed so" (V.ii.193). Perhaps Lucentio implies that Kate and Petruccio planned the wager, and that they worked as a team to dupe the others out of their money. Throughout the play, Kate actively accepted Petruccio's courting and taming even when she could have denied him, suggesting that here she also has the agency to say one thing and mean another. Despite her initial resistance, Kate seems to view her marriage as a chance to find harmony within a prescribed social role, ultimately implying that we should find happiness and independence within the roles to which we are assigned, not that women should subjugate themselves to men.

Lucentio's marriage takes a different turn, however. Through Bianca's refusal to come when called, Shakespeare suggests that this marriage will be hard on Lucentio. Bianca might turn out to be as stubborn in her role as a wife as she was mild in her role as a maid. Thus, in his last few lines, Petruccio observes, "We three are married, but you two are sped" (V.ii.189). That is, the other two—Lucentio and Hortensio—seem destined for unhappiness in marriage, given the disobedient natures of their wives. Petruccio fought tooth and nail to finally win Kate, but he worked hard only because he wanted her to truly allow herself to accept, or choose, obedience in married life. Lucentio, deceived by Bianca's meekness and flirtatious behavior when they were single, now finds that it is "a harsh hearing when women are froward" (V.ii.187).

IMPORTANT QUOTATIONS EXPLAINED

1. Signor Hortensio, 'twixt such friends as we
    Few words suffice; and therefore, if thou know
    One rich enough to be Petruccio's wife—
    As wealth is burden of my wooing dance—
    Be she as foul as was Florentius' love,
    As old as Sibyl, and as curst and shrewd
    As Socrates' Xanthippe or a worse,
    She moves me not—or not removes at least
    Affection's edge in me, were she as rough
    As are the swelling Adriatic seas.
    I come to wive it wealthily in Padua;
    If wealthily, then happily in Padua.

    (I.ii.62–73)

Petruccio speaks these lines to Hortensio to explain his intention of finding a bride in Padua. He frankly states that his main goal is to marry for money, equating wedding with wealthy results—that is, marrying a rich wife—with wedding happily. Apart from his prospective wife's wealth, Petruccio says that he does not care about any of her other qualities. He says that the woman may be as "foul as was Florentius' love," referring to a story in which the knight Florent was forced to marry an old woman who saved his life. She may be as "old as Sibyl," a mythic prophetess who lived forever, but who continued to grow older and older. Or she may be as unpleasant as "Socrates' Xanthippe," a woman traditionally reputed to be a great shrew. Indeed, she may be any or all of these things, and Petruccio cares not so long as she is rich. This speech exemplifies Petruccio's brash, robust manner of speaking. He is blatantly honest about his materialism and selfishness, and he also straightforwardly acknowledges the economic aspect of marriage—something that everyone in the play is keenly aware of but which only Petruccio discusses so frankly and openly and with so little concern for romantic love.

2.   PETRUCCIO: Come, come, you wasp, i'faith you are
                                too angry.
      KATHERINE: If I be waspish, best beware my sting.
      PETRUCCIO: My remedy is then to pluck it out.
      KATHERINE: Ay, if the fool could find where it lies.
      PETRUCCIO: Who knows not where a wasp does wear
                                his sting?In his tail.
      KATHERINE: In his tongue.
      PETRUCCIO: Whose tongue?
      KATHERINE: Yours, if you talk of tales, and so farewell.
      PETRUCCIO: What, with my tongue in your tail?
                                (II.i.207–214)

This exchange between the two main characters occurs during their first meeting. Their conversation is an extraordinary display of verbal wit, with Petruccio making use of lurid sexual puns in order to undermine Katherine's standoffishness and anger. Other characters frequently compare Katherine to a dangerous wild animal, and in this case, Petruccio calls her a wasp. She replies angrily that if she is a wasp, he had better beware her sting. He replies confidently that he will simply pluck her sting out, rendering her unable to harm him. In saying this, Petruccio basically throws down a challenge to Katherine, acknowledging his intent to tame her. Katherine, disgusted, says that Petruccio is too much of a fool even to know where a wasp's sting is. Katherine's comment refers to her sharp tongue, but Petruccio turns her statement into a sexual innuendo by insisting that a wasp wears his sting in his tail. Katherine then hastily contradicts him and says, "In his tongue."

Katherine refers to wasps that bite, and Petruccio makes reference to bees that have stingers in their abdomens. Katherine's metaphor implies that she will sting him with her wit, but Petruccio's metaphor implies that he will "pluck out" the stinger from Katherine's "tail," a reference to her genitals. When Petruccio asks "Whose tongue?" Katherine replies, "Yours, if you talk of tales," implying that if he continues to pursue her, she will sting him on his tongue, painfully. But Petruccio again turns this into a sexual image, pretending to be surprised at the picture of "my tongue in your tail." This passage embodies not only the fiery conflict between Petruccio and Katherine, but also the sexual attraction underlying it. It also extends the play's ruling motif of domestication, as Petruccio yet again describes Katherine as a wild animal that he will tame.

QUOTATIONS

3. Thus in plain terms: your father hath consented
    That you shall be my wife, your dowry 'greed on,
    And will you, nill you, I will marry you.
    Now Kate, I am a husband for your turn,
    For by this light, whereby I see thy beauty—
    Thy beauty that doth make me like thee well—
    Thou must be married to no man but me,
    For I am he am born to tame you, Kate,
    And bring you from a wild Kate to a Kate
    Conformable as other household Kates.
    Here comes your father. Never make denial.
    I must and will have Katherine to my wife.

                                    (II.i.261–272)

Petruccio speaks these lines to Katherine shortly after his "my tongue in your tail" comment (see above). Petruccio confronts the reluctant Katherine with his intentions: since her father has agreed and the dowry has been settled, he will marry her whether she likes it or not ("will you, nill you, I will marry you"). Petruccio even explicitly declares that "I am he am born to tame you, Kate," further employing the language of animal domestication by calling her a "wild Kate"—a pun on "wildcat"—that he will "tame." Not only does this speech set the terms for Petruccio and Katherine's later relationship, but it is also important for what immediately follows: Katherine, fully aware of Petruccio's intentions, implicitly consents to marry him by failing to protest against his false claims that she has already agreed to do so.

4.   Then God be blessed, it is the blessed sun,
       But sun it is not when you say it is not,
       And the moon changes even as your mind.
       What you will have it named, even that it is,
       And so it shall be still for Katherine.

                                              (IV.vi.19–23)

Katherine makes this contrite speech after Petruccio orders her to say that the sun is really the moon. Tired, hungry, and weary of their conflicts, Katherine at last relents and declares that, for all she cares, Petruccio might as well define reality for her from this point forward. In terms of Kate's consciousness, even celestial events and objects submit to Petruccio's will. With this, Petruccio's victory over Katherine becomes inevitable: after this, she can resist his authority only halfheartedly, and her taming is nearly complete.

5.   Thy husband is thy lord, thy life, thy keeper,
Thy head, thy sovereign, one that cares for thee,
And for thy maintenance commits his body
To painful labour both by sea and land,
To watch the night in storms, the day in cold,
Whilst thou liest warm at home, secure and safe,
And craves no other tribute at thy hands
But love, fair looks, and true obedience,
Too little payment for so great a debt.

. . .

My mind hath been as big as one of yours,
My heart as great, my reason haply more,
To bandy word for word and frown for frown;
But now I see our lances are but straws,
Our strength as weak, our weakness past compare,
That seeming to be most which we indeed least are.
Then vail your stomachs, for it is no boot,
And place your hands below your husband's foot,
In token of which duty, if he please,
My hand is ready, may it do him ease.

(V.ii.140–183)

Kate makes this long speech at the end of the play. It indicates a
shocking transformation of her opinions about marriage and men,
and it stuns everyone who hears it. The once shrewish Katherine
now declares that Bianca and Hortensio's widow are ingrates for
looking angrily at their husbands—whom Katherine describes as
their lords, kings, and governors. She says that a woman's husband
protects her and supports her, living a life of danger and responsibility while the woman is "warm at home, secure and safe." In return,
she says that the husband asks only for his wife's kindness and obedience, which represents but tiny payment for "so great a debt." A
husband is to his wife as a prince is to his subject, and if a woman
proves shrewish ("froward, peevish, sullen, sour"), then she is like a
traitor to a just ruler.

    Katherine says that women's bodies are soft and weak because
their inner selves should match them and that women should thus
yield to their men. She then tells Bianca and the widow that, in her
time, she has been as proud and as headstrong as they are ("My
mind hath been as big as one of yours, / My heart as great"), but
now she understands that "our lances are but straws," implying

that their weapons prove insignificant and improperly used. A woman should prepare herself to do anything for her husband, including, as Katherine does now, kneel before him and hold his foot. This speech indicates the extent of Katherine's character development over the course of the play—she began the play by fighting against her social role, but now she offers a forty-three-line defense of it. The speech also summarizes the play's view of marital harmony, in which husbands provide peace, security, and comfort to their wives, who, in return, provide loyalty and obedience.

KEY FACTS

FULL TITLE
The Taming of the Shrew

AUTHOR
William Shakespeare

TYPE OF WORK
Play

GENRE
Romantic comedy

LANGUAGE
English

TIME AND PLACE WRITTEN
Around 1592, London

DATE OF FIRST PUBLICATION
1623

TONE
The overall tone of the play is light and comic, though the exploration of larger social questions, such as the proper relation of the sexes in marriage, lends much of the comedy a more serious tone.

SETTINGS (TIME)
Unspecific, though presumably sometime during the Italian Renaissance

SETTINGS (PLACE)
Padua, a city-state in Italy prominent during the Renaissance

PROTAGONIST
There is no single protagonist; Katherine and Petruccio are the main characters.

MAJOR CONFLICT
Petruccio's attempt to "tame" Katherine; that is, to assert his authority in their marriage and overcome her hotheaded resistance to playing the role of his wife

RISING ACTION

Petruccio and Katherine's early verbal conflicts; Katherine's many scenes of shrewish behavior, including her attack on Bianca; the various disguises and subterfuges of the subplot; Katherine and Petruccio's comical wedding

CLIMAX

There is no single moment of intense action in the play, but rather a long process of development culminating in Katherine's fully changed behavior. It might be possible to see a climax in the wedding scene in Act III, or in Katherine's decision in Act IV to submit to Petruccio when he says the sun is really the moon, or her agreement to throw shame to the winds and kiss him in the middle of the street in Act IV.

FALLING ACTION

The banquet at Lucentio's house in Act V, scene ii

THEMES

Marriage as an economic institution; the effect of social roles on individual happiness

MOTIFS

Disguise; domestication; fathers and their children

SYMBOLS

Petruccio's wedding costume; the haberdasher's cap and tailor's gown

FORESHADOWING

Petruccio's declaration to Katherine in Act II that he is the man to tame her

STUDY QUESTIONS & ESSAY TOPICS

STUDY QUESTIONS

1. *Disguise plays a crucial role in* The Taming of the Shrew, *throughout both the Induction and the main story. While most of the disguises are removed in the end, those who use them to achieve a specified goal generally succeed— particularly Lucentio and Tranio. What can we infer about Shakespeare's take on the effects of disguise? Can clothes really make the man?*

Disguise in *The Taming of the Shrew* enables characters to temporarily change their social positions. By donning a disguise, Lucentio transforms himself in the eyes of everyone around him from a young gentleman into a scholar, and Tranio transforms himself from a servant into an aristocrat. Clothing facilitates this effect because outward appearance controls the perceptions of others: because Tranio appears to be a gentleman, people treat him as a gentleman. However, as Petruccio says, no matter what a person wears, his inner self will eventually shine through—Lucentio, for instance, may appear to be a tutor, but as soon as the courtship with Bianca develops, he must revert to himself again. Additionally, one cannot escape one's past simply by changing one's clothes. People are bound together in intricate webs and, interwoven as such, cannot escape their identity. The webs tend to reveal true selves regardless of attire or intent—a point that Shakespeare illustrates when Vincentio encounters Tranio in disguise.

QUESTIONS & ESSAYS

2.   *The Induction plays a mysterious role in the play. In fact, we never see the conclusion of the trick played on Christopher Sly. What is the purpose of the Induction, structurally, narratively, or thematically? In the end, does the Induction serve merely a cursory role in introducing the play proper, or does it provide commentary on the themes throughout?*

Many of Shakespeare's dramas utilize the concept of "plays within plays," in which characters in the play attend the performance of another play; prominent examples include the "Mousetrap" scene in *Hamlet* and the "Pyramus and Thisbe" scene at the end of *A Midsummer Night's Dream*. But *The Taming of the Shrew* is unique in that the "play within a play" is the main play: the story of Petruccio and Kate is presented as a play viewed by the otherwise insignificant character of Christopher Sly. The Induction, the section at the beginning of the play that introduces Sly, may be narratively unsatisfying, especially as we are not privy to the conclusion of Sly's story. However, the Induction incorporates many of the major motifs of the main play, such as that of disguise. Sly's identity changes when his clothes are changed, just as Lucentio's does. Sly must act according to the role in which he finds himself, just as Kate must. Finally, Sly is interested in having a wife over whom he can hold sway, just as most of the male characters in the main story are.

3. *What techniques does Petruccio employ to "tame"*
    Katherine? Why do they work? Is Petruccio's
    manipulation of Kate plausible?

Petruccio uses a number of different techniques to "tame" Kate: he proves to her that he can match her verbal acuity and quick wit, then he wields his extreme confidence, and his status as a man, when he boldly tells her father that she has already agreed to marry him when, in fact, she has not. At the wedding, he humiliates her by wearing absurd clothing, arriving late, and riding a broken-down horse, and then he exerts his authority over her by forcing her to leave immediately. When they reach his house, he decides to "kill [her] with kindness," pretending he cannot allow her to eat his inferior food or sleep on his inferior bed because he cares for her greatly. As a result, she grows tired and hungry and must depend on Petruccio's goodwill to fulfill her needs, reinforcing in her mind the idea that he controls her. Because Petruccio couches his attempt to tame Kate in the rhetoric of love and affection, it is impossible for her to confront him with outright anger, and the possibility remains that the two will develop a genuinely loving relationship in the future. Of course, *The Taming of the Shrew* is a comedy, and Petruccio's techniques are somewhat fantastical. But both Kate's apparent willingness to comply with Petruccio's demands and Petruccio's desire to court Kate's love make considerably more logical sense if we accept the explanation that, beneath their conflicts, they legitimately love one another.

QUESTIONS & ESSAYS

SUGGESTED ESSAY TOPICS

1. How do gender roles affect the attitudes of the characters, and how do these roles surface in the play? Most of the men seem to have a particular idea about how a wife should behave, but do their preconceptions extend to all women? How do the women react to these expectations? Are the women systematically oppressed, or do they subtly balance the men's power?

2. The play is essentially a comedy, and yet more serious questions about social issues often overshadow its comic features. How does humor function in *The Taming of the Shrew*? Note especially the two wooing scenes, by Petruccio (Act II, scene i) and Lucentio (Act III, scene i). Why does Shakespeare include so many of the play's best comic devices in these scenes?

3. Examine the characters of Hortensio and Gremio. Why do they fail where Petruccio and Lucentio succeed? Does their failure stem from their reasons for wanting to get married or from other facets of their personalities?

4. In general, the plots of Shakespeare's plays follow a certain pattern, in which Act III contains a major turning point in the action and events that "inevitably" lead to the climax of action and the wrap-up of plot lines in the fifth and final act. How does *The Taming of The Shrew* conform to, or deviate from, this pattern? How substantially do the events of the third act—the marriage scene between Petruccio and Kate, and the wooing scene between Lucentio and Bianca—affect the action of the rest of the play?

Review & Resources

Quiz

1.   Which character is late for Katherine and Petruccio's wedding?

     A.   Petruccio
     B.   Biondello
     C.   The pedant
     D.   Baptista

2.   Who becomes Bianca's music teacher?

     A.   Gremio
     B.   Lucentio
     C.   Hortensio
     D.   Grumio

3.   Which character is Petruccio's servant?

     A.   Gremio
     B.   Grumio
     C.   Biondello
     D.   Hortensio

4.   How does Lucentio declare his love for Bianca?

     A.   Through a clever music lesson
     B.   Through a sonnet he leaves on her pillow
     C.   By whispering in her ear
     D.   Through a Latin translation

5.   Where is most of the play set?

     A.   Padua
     B.   Verona
     C.   Venice
     D.   Warwickshire

6. Whom does Baptista believe to be Lucentio for most of the play?

    A.   Lucentio
    B.   Hortensio
    C.   Biondello
    D.   Tranio

7. How does Petruccio prevent Kate from eating after their marriage?

    A.   He tells her she is too fat.
    B.   He says that the food is not good enough for her.
    C.   He simply forbids her.
    D.   He tells her that the food is poisoned.

8. What does Petruccio convince Kate to say about the sun?

    A.   That it is black
    B.   That it is too dim
    C.   That it is cold
    D.   That it is the moon

9. What is Christopher Sly's profession?

    A.   Tinker
    B.   Tailor
    C.   Soldier
    D.   Spy

10. Who is Bianca's father?

    A.   Tranio
    B.   Gremio
    C.   Baptista
    D.   Petruccio

11. Who tricks Sly?

    A.   A knight
    B.   A lord
    C.   A king
    D.   A priest

12. Who pretends to be Lucentio's father?

   A. Baptista
   B. Vincentio
   C. Biondello
   D. The pedant

13. Who convinces Bianca and Lucentio to elope?

   A. Biondello
   B. Cherubino
   C. The pedant
   D. Vincentio

14. Whose wife is the first to answer the summons at the end of the play?

   A. Baptista's
   B. Hortensio's
   C. Petruccio's
   D. Lucentio's

15. How does Tranio trick the pedant?

   A. He tells him that pedants are illegal in Padua.
   B. He tells him that Padua and Mantua are at war.
   C. He tells him that his twin brother has robbed St. Christopher's.
   D. He tells him that his daughter is dressing as a man.

16. Who becomes Bianca's Latin teacher?

   A. Tranio
   B. Hortensio
   C. Grumio
   D. Lucentio

17. How does Petruccio set his wedding date?

   A. He asks Kate when she would like to be married.
   B. He falsely claims that Kate has agreed to marry him on Sunday.
   C. He consults Baptista.
   D. He consults Biondello.

REVIEW & RESOURCES

18. What is a "shrew," as defined by this play?

    A.   A burrowing creature that often ruined Italian gardens
    B.   A chauvinistic and overbearing man
    C.   An ill-tempered and disobedient woman
    D.   An old man who tries to marry a young girl

19. Why does Petruccio agree to marry Kate?

    A.   He wants her father's money.
    B.   He likes her personality.
    C.   He is desperately lonely.
    D.   He is drunk.

20. What object of the haberdasher's does Kate covet?

    A.   A wedding gown
    B.   Gloves
    C.   A dressmaker's dummy
    D.   A hat

21. Does Petruccio give it to her?

    A.   Yes
    B.   No

22. Whom do Petruccio and Kate meet on the road back to Padua?

    A.   Tranio
    B.   Vincentio
    C.   Lucentio
    D.   Bianca and Lucentio

23. Whom does Hortensio marry?

    A.   Bianca
    B.   Kate
    C.   A wealthy widow
    D.   No one

24. Where do Petruccio and Kate go at the end of the play?

   A. To bed
   B. To Rome
   C. To London
   D. To Verona

25. How are Bianca and Kate related?

   A.   They are cousins.
   B.   Bianca is Kate's daughter.
   C.   Kate is Bianca's niece.
   D.   They are sisters.

ANSWER KEY:
1: A; 2: C; 3: B; 4: D; 5: A; 6: D; 7: B; 8: D; 9: A; 10: C; 11:
B; 12: D; 13: A; 14: C; 15: B; 16: D; 17: B; 18: C; 19: A; 20:
D; 21: B; 22: B; 23: C; 24: A; 25: D

SUGGESTIONS FOR FURTHER READING

BOUGHNER, DANIEL C. *The Braggart in Renaissance Comedy.* Minneapolis: University of Minnesota Press, 1954.

BRINK, JEAN R., MARYANNE C. HOROWITZ, AND ALLISON P. COUDERT, EDS. *Playing with Gender: A Renaissance Pursuit.* Urbana: University of Illinois Press, 1991.

CAMDEN, CHARLES CARROLL. *The Elizabethan Woman.* London: Cleavery-Hume, 1952.

DOLAN, FRANCES E. *The Taming of the Shrew: Texts and Contexts.* New York: Bedford Books of St. Martin's Press, 1996.

NEWMAN, KAREN. *"Renaissance Family Politics and Shakespeare's Taming of the Shrew." In Fashioning Femininity and English Renaissance Drama.* Chicago: University of Chicago Press, 1991.

SWISHER, CLARICE, BRUNO LEONE, AND SCOTT BARBOUR, EDS. *Readings on the Comedies of William Shakespeare.* San Diego: Greenhaven Press, 1997.

UNDERDOWN, DAVID. *"The Taming of the Scold: The Enforcement of Patriarchal Authority in Early Modern England." in Order and Disorder in Early Modern England, eds.* Anthony Fletcher and John Stevenson. Cambridge: Cambridge University Press, 1985.

REVIEW & RESOURCES

A Note on the Type

The typeface used in SparkNotes study guides is Sabon, created by master typographer Jan Tschichold in 1964. Tschichold revolutionized the field of graphic design twice: first with his use of asymmetrical layouts and sanserif type in the 1930s when he was affiliated with the Bauhaus, then by abandoning assymetry and calling for a return to the classic ideals of design. Sabon, his only extant typeface, is emblematic of his latter program: Tschichold's design is a recreation of the types made by Claude Garamond, the great French typographer of the Renaissance, and his contemporary Robert Granjon. Fittingly, it is named for Garamond's apprentice, Jacques Sabon.

SPARKNOTES TEST PREPARATION GUIDES

The SparkNotes team figured it was time to cut standardized tests down to size. We've studied the tests for you, so that SparkNotes test prep guides are:

Smarter:
Packed with critical-thinking skills and test-
taking strategies that will improve your score.

Better:
Fully up to date, covering all new features of the tests,
with study tips on every type of question.

Faster:
Our books cover exactly what you need to
know for the test. No more, no less.

SparkNotes Guide to the SAT & PSAT
SparkNotes Guide to the SAT & PSAT—Deluxe Internet Edition
SparkNotes Guide to the ACT
SparkNotes Guide to the ACT—Deluxe Internet Edition
SparkNotes Guide to the SAT II Writing
SparkNotes Guide to the SAT II U.S. History
SparkNotes Guide to the SAT II Math Ic
SparkNotes Guide to the SAT II Math IIc
SparkNotes Guide to the SAT II Biology
SparkNotes Guide to the SAT II Physics

SAT and PSAT are registered trademarks of the College Entrance Examination Board, which does not endorse these books.
ACT is a registered trademark of ACT, Inc. which neither sponsors nor endorses these books.

SparkNotes Study Guides: